The Power Within: Embracing Personal Strengths and Igniting Your Passions

Brittany

Copyright © [2023]

Title: The Power Within: Embracing Personal Strengths and Igniting Your Passions

Author's: **Brittany**

All rights reserved. No part of this publication may be reproduced, stored in a retrieval system, or transmitted in any form or by any means, electronic, mechanical, photocopying, recording, or otherwise, without the prior written permission of the publisher or author, except in the case of brief quotations embodied in critical reviews and certain other non-commercial uses permitted by copyright law.

This book was printed and published by [Publisher's: **Brittany**] in [2023]

ISBN:

TABLE OF CONTENT

Chapter 1: Discovering Your Personal Strengths and Passions   08

Understanding Personal Strengths

Identifying Your Natural Talents

Recognizing Skills You Have Developed

Discovering Strengths through Experience

Uncovering Your Passions

Exploring Activities That Excite You

Reflecting on What Brings You Joy

Finding Meaning and Purpose in Your Passions

Chapter 2: Embracing and Cultivating Your Personal Strengths 24

Accepting and Celebrating Your Strengths

Embracing Your Unique Qualities

Overcoming Self-Doubt and Comparison

Gratitude for Your Strengths

Developing and Expanding Your Strengths

Setting Goals to Enhance Your Strengths

Seeking Opportunities for Growth

Building a Supportive Network

Chapter 3: Nurturing Your Passions   **40**

Making Time for Your Passions

Prioritizing Your Interests

Incorporating Passion into Your Daily Life

Balancing Responsibilities and Pursuits

Fueling Your Passions

Learning and Gaining Knowledge

Seeking Inspiration from Others

Taking Risks and Embracing Challenges

Chapter 4: Igniting Your Passions and Achieving Success 56

Setting Goals Aligned with Your Passions

Defining Clear and Measurable Goals

Creating a Plan of Action

Tracking Progress and Making Adjustments

Overcoming Obstacles and Persevering

Dealing with Fear and Failure

Building Resilience and Determination

Seeking Support and Encouragement

Chapter 5: Living a Fulfilling Life through Personal Strengths and Passions   72

Embracing Growth and Continuous Learning

Cultivating a Growth Mindset

Embracing New Opportunities and Challenges

Seeking Feedback for Improvement

Inspiring Others through Your Journey

Sharing Your Story and Experiences

Mentoring and Supporting Others

Encouraging Self-Discovery and Personal Growth

Conclusion: Unleashing the Power Within You   88

Chapter 1: Discovering Your Personal Strengths and Passions

Understanding Personal Strengths

In the journey of self-discovery and personal growth, one of the most important aspects is understanding and embracing our personal strengths. Each one of us possesses unique qualities and abilities that contribute to our individuality and potential for success. However, many individuals struggle to recognize their own strengths and often overlook the power they hold within themselves. This subchapter aims to help you explore and understand your personal strengths, allowing you to ignite your passions and live a more fulfilling life.

To truly discover your personal strengths, it is crucial to start by looking within. Take the time for self-reflection and introspection. Consider your past accomplishments and moments where you felt confident and empowered. These instances often highlight your natural talents and abilities. Evaluate the activities that bring you joy and fulfillment. What are the skills required for these activities? These skills are likely your personal strengths.

Furthermore, seeking feedback from others can provide valuable insights into your strengths. Ask your friends, family, and colleagues about the qualities they admire in you. Their observations can shed light on attributes that you may not have recognized in yourself. Additionally, consider taking personality assessments or working with a career coach who can guide you in identifying your personal strengths.

It is important to remember that personal strengths come in various forms. They can be cognitive, emotional, social, or physical. Some individuals may excel in logical thinking and problem-solving, while others possess exceptional empathy and emotional intelligence. These strengths can be further developed and applied to different areas of your life, whether personal or professional.

Once you have identified your personal strengths, it is essential to embrace them fully. Recognize that your strengths are not weaknesses and that they set you apart from others. Cultivate a positive mindset, focusing on your strengths rather than dwelling on perceived shortcomings. Celebrate your achievements and use your strengths to overcome challenges and accomplish your goals.

Understanding and embracing your personal strengths can be a transformative experience. It allows you to tap into your full potential, build self-confidence, and find fulfillment in every aspect of your life. By recognizing and utilizing your strengths, you will have the power to create positive change, not only within yourself but also in the world around you. Embrace your personal strengths, ignite your passions, and unlock the power within you.

Identifying Your Natural Talents

We all possess unique talents that make us special and capable of achieving great things in life. However, many of us fail to recognize or fully utilize these inherent abilities. In this subchapter, we will delve into the process of identifying your natural talents and how to harness them to find the good within you.

Finding the good in yourself begins with self-reflection and self-awareness. Take a moment to ponder upon your strengths and abilities. What activities or tasks do you excel at effortlessly? What brings you joy and satisfaction? These are the clues that will help unveil your natural talents.

Sometimes, your talents may be ingrained so deeply within you that they become almost invisible. If this is the case, it can be helpful to seek feedback from others. Ask your friends, family, or colleagues about their perceptions of your strengths and what they believe you excel at. Often, the people around us can provide valuable insights that we may have overlooked.

Additionally, pay attention to activities that energize you and make you lose track of time. These are the moments when you are in a state of flow, fully engaged and utilizing your natural talents. Identifying these moments will help you understand what truly ignites your passions.

It is important to note that natural talents are not limited to traditional skills like playing an instrument or painting. They can also manifest in areas such as problem-solving, empathy, leadership, or communication. Each person has a unique combination of talents that sets them apart from others.

Once you have identified your natural talents, it is crucial to nurture and develop them. Seek opportunities to further enhance your skills through practice, training, or education. Remember, talent alone is not enough; it requires continuous effort and dedication to reach its full potential.

Embracing your natural talents can lead to a life filled with purpose, fulfillment, and success. By recognizing and utilizing your strengths, you can unlock your true potential and make a positive impact in both your personal and professional life.

In conclusion, identifying your natural talents is a vital step towards finding the good within you. Through self-reflection, seeking feedback, and recognizing moments of flow, you can uncover your unique abilities. Once discovered, these talents must be nurtured and developed to reach their full potential. Embrace your natural talents, ignite your passions, and unleash the power within you.

Recognizing Skills You Have Developed

In a society that often emphasizes self-improvement and constantly striving for success, it is easy to overlook the skills and strengths that we have already developed. However, recognizing and acknowledging these skills is crucial in finding the good within ourselves and embracing our personal strengths. In this subchapter, we will explore the importance of recognizing the skills that you have developed and how they can ignite your passions.

Often, we tend to focus on our weaknesses and the areas where we feel inadequate. This negative mindset can hinder our personal growth and prevent us from fully embracing our potential. By shifting our attention to the skills we have acquired over time, we open ourselves up to a world of possibilities and opportunities.

The first step in recognizing the skills you have developed is to take a moment for introspection. Reflect on your past experiences, both personal and professional, and identify the tasks and responsibilities that you excelled at. Consider the feedback you have received from others and the accomplishments you have achieved. These experiences and achievements are a testament to the skills you possess.

Next, it is important to understand that skills come in various forms. They can be technical skills, such as proficiency in a particular software or expertise in a specific field. However, skills can also be interpersonal, such as effective communication, leadership, or problem-solving abilities. By broadening our definition of skills, we can uncover hidden talents and strengths that we may have overlooked.

Recognizing the skills you have developed not only boosts your self-confidence but also helps you discover your passions. By understanding what you excel at, you can align your goals and aspirations with your natural abilities. This alignment creates a sense of fulfillment and purpose, as you are utilizing your skills in areas that truly ignite your passion.

Remember, recognizing your developed skills is not about comparing yourself to others or seeking validation from external sources. It is about acknowledging your unique strengths and talents, and embracing them as a part of your authentic self. By recognizing and celebrating the skills you have developed, you can unlock the power within you to achieve your dreams and live a more fulfilling life.

In conclusion, recognizing the skills you have developed is a crucial step in finding the good within yourself. By shifting your focus from weaknesses to strengths, you open yourself up to a world of possibilities and opportunities. Take the time to reflect on your past experiences, identify your accomplishments, and broaden your definition of skills. By recognizing and embracing your skills, you can align your goals with your passions and live a more fulfilling life. Remember, the power to embrace your personal strengths lies within you.

Discovering Strengths through Experience

In our journey through life, we often encounter moments of self-doubt and uncertainty. We question our abilities and wonder if we have what it takes to succeed. However, buried deep within each one of us lies a wealth of untapped potential and hidden strengths waiting to be discovered. It is through our experiences, both positive and negative, that we can truly uncover the power within ourselves.

The subchapter "Discovering Strengths through Experience" in the book "The Power Within: Embracing Personal Strengths and Igniting Your Passions" aims to guide every individual on a transformative journey of self-discovery. Whether you are a student, a working professional, or someone seeking personal growth, this subchapter is designed to help you find the good within yourself.

One of the first steps towards discovering your strengths is reflection. Take a moment to pause and reflect on your life experiences. What challenges have you faced? What obstacles have you overcome? These experiences, no matter how big or small, have shaped you into the person you are today. By understanding the lessons learned from these experiences, you can uncover your unique strengths and abilities.

Another important aspect of discovering strengths is embracing failures. Often, we view failures as setbacks or signs of weakness. However, failures are valuable learning opportunities that can help us grow and develop. By reframing our perspective and viewing failures as stepping stones towards success, we can unlock new strengths and resilience within ourselves.

Furthermore, seeking feedback from others can provide valuable insights into our strengths. Reach out to trusted mentors, friends, or family members and ask them for their honest assessment of your skills and abilities. Their perspectives may shed light on hidden strengths that you might have overlooked.

Lastly, don't be afraid to step out of your comfort zone and try new things. Engaging in different activities and experiences allows you to discover talents and interests you never knew existed. Trying new hobbies, taking up new challenges, or volunteering for unfamiliar tasks can open doors to previously undiscovered strengths and passions.

Ultimately, discovering strengths through experience is a lifelong journey. It requires self-reflection, embracing failures, seeking feedback, and stepping out of your comfort zone. By actively engaging in this process, you will unlock the power within yourself and find the good that has always been present. Embrace your uniqueness, embrace your strengths, and let them guide you towards a life filled with purpose and fulfillment.

Uncovering Your Passions

In the journey of self-discovery, one of the most fulfilling and essential aspects is uncovering your passions. Often, we find ourselves lost and disconnected from our true selves, struggling to identify what truly makes us happy and fulfilled. However, within each and every one of us lies a vast reservoir of untapped potential and hidden passions waiting to be explored.

This subchapter of "The Power Within: Embracing Personal Strengths and Igniting Your Passions" is dedicated to guiding you on the path towards finding the good within yourself and unearthing those passions that will bring you joy and purpose.

The first step towards uncovering your passions is self-reflection. Take the time to pause, disconnect from the noise of the world, and delve deep into your thoughts and emotions. Ask yourself what truly excites you, what activities bring you a sense of fulfillment, and what makes you lose track of time. These clues will lead you towards your passions.

It is important to remember that passion is not solely limited to grand ambitions or extraordinary talents. It can be found in the simplest of activities or hobbies. Whether it's cooking, painting, gardening, or even organizing, your passion is unique to you. Embrace it, for it is the key to unlocking your true potential.

Another valuable tool in uncovering your passions is exploration. Step out of your comfort zone and try new things. Engage in activities that pique your curiosity and challenge you. Attend workshops, join clubs, or volunteer for causes that align with your values. These experiences will expose you to new perspectives and help you discover what truly resonates with your soul.

Moreover, surround yourself with supportive people who encourage and inspire you. Seek out mentors or join communities of like-minded individuals who share your interests. Their guidance and encouragement will fuel your journey towards discovering and embracing your passions.

Lastly, be patient and kind to yourself. Uncovering your passions is a process that takes time and self-acceptance. Do not compare your journey to others', as everyone's path is unique. Embrace your strengths and weaknesses, for they are all part of the tapestry that makes you who you are.

Remember, within you lies a universe of untapped potential and hidden passions. Embrace this subchapter as a guide to uncovering your passions and igniting the power within. Go forth with an open heart and mind, and let the journey of self-discovery unfold before you.

Exploring Activities That Excite You

In the journey of self-discovery and personal growth, it is essential to explore activities that excite and ignite your passions. When you engage in activities that resonate with your inner self, you not only find joy and fulfillment but also unlock your true potential. This subchapter aims to guide you in identifying and embracing activities that bring out the best in you.

Finding the good within yourself starts by recognizing your unique strengths and passions. We all possess a set of skills and abilities that make us stand out from the crowd. Take some time to reflect on what activities make you feel alive, motivated, and truly happy. Pursuing these activities will not only enhance your overall well-being but also provide you with a sense of purpose and direction in life.

One way to explore activities that resonate with you is through self-reflection. Consider the moments in your life when you felt the most fulfilled and engaged. Was it when you were painting, playing an instrument, solving complex problems, or helping others? Pay attention to these instances as they provide invaluable insights into your true passions.

Another approach is to try new things and step out of your comfort zone. Often, we limit ourselves to the familiar, fearing the unknown. However, by venturing into uncharted territories, you open yourself up to a world of possibilities. Attend workshops, join clubs or groups, or simply experiment with different hobbies. You may be surprised to discover new interests that ignite your passions and bring you a renewed sense of enthusiasm.

Moreover, seeking inspiration from others can be a powerful tool in finding activities that excite you. Observe people who radiate joy and fulfillment in their pursuits. Engage in conversations with them, understand their journey, and learn from their experiences. Their stories can serve as a guiding light, helping you uncover hidden talents and passions within yourself.

Remember, exploring activities that excite you is not only about finding external sources of happiness but also about connecting with your inner self. It is about aligning your passions with your values and beliefs, allowing you to live a life that is authentic and true to yourself.

In conclusion, the subchapter "Exploring Activities That Excite You" encourages you to embark on a journey of self-discovery and find the activities that bring out the best in you. By recognizing your strengths, reflecting on past moments of fulfillment, trying new things, and seeking inspiration from others, you will uncover passions that ignite your personal power. Embrace these activities, align them with your values, and let them guide you towards a life of joy, purpose, and fulfillment.

Reflecting on What Brings You Joy

In our fast-paced and often chaotic lives, it is crucial to take a moment to reflect on what truly brings us joy. In this subchapter, we will explore the importance of finding the good within ourselves and the power it holds to transform our lives.

Finding joy is not always an easy task, especially when we are bombarded with negativity from various sources. However, when we take the time to reflect and focus on the positive aspects of our lives, we can experience a profound shift in our mindset and overall well-being.

One of the first steps in discovering what brings you joy is to cultivate self-awareness. Self-awareness enables you to recognize your strengths, passions, and personal preferences. By understanding yourself on a deeper level, you can better identify the activities, experiences, and relationships that truly ignite your inner spark.

When you engage in activities that bring you joy, you tap into your personal strengths and talents. These are the unique skills and abilities that make you who you are. Embracing and utilizing your strengths can lead to a sense of fulfillment and accomplishment. It is through this process that you can uncover your true potential and make a positive impact in your own life and the lives of others.

Reflecting on what brings you joy also involves acknowledging and embracing your passions. Passion is the fuel that drives us to pursue our dreams and goals. It is the fire that ignites our creativity and propels us forward. When we align our actions with our passions, we experience a sense of purpose and fulfillment that cannot be replicated.

In this subchapter, we will provide practical exercises and strategies to help you reflect on what brings you joy. We will guide you through introspective activities that will enable you to identify your strengths, passions, and the positive aspects of your life. Additionally, we will discuss the importance of incorporating joy into your daily routine and how it can positively impact your overall well-being.

Remember, everyone has the power within to find joy and embrace their personal strengths. By reflecting on what brings you joy, you can uncover a world of possibilities and create a life filled with purpose, happiness, and fulfillment. So, let us embark on this transformative journey together and discover the incredible power within you!

Finding Meaning and Purpose in Your Passions

In a world that often feels chaotic and overwhelming, it is crucial to find meaning and purpose in our lives. Many of us spend our days searching for happiness and fulfillment, but often overlook the power of our own passions. In this subchapter, we will explore the importance of finding the good within ourselves and how we can harness our passions to create a more meaningful life.

Passions are the fuel that ignites our souls and brings us joy. They are the activities and interests that make our hearts sing and fill us with a sense of purpose. Whether it is writing, painting, gardening, or any other form of creative expression, these passions are unique to each individual. They are the threads that weave together the tapestry of our identities.

When we tap into our passions and invest time and energy in them, we begin to uncover the hidden gems within ourselves. We discover talents and strengths that we may not have even known existed. The act of engaging in our passions allows us to access a deep well of personal strength that can propel us forward in all areas of our lives.

Finding meaning and purpose in our passions also helps us to connect with others on a deeper level. When we share our passions with the world, we inspire and uplift those around us. Our passions have the power to touch the lives of others and create a ripple effect of positivity. By embracing our personal strengths and igniting our passions, we become beacons of light and hope in a world that often feels dim.

However, finding meaning and purpose in our passions is not always an easy journey. It requires self-reflection, exploration, and a willingness to step outside of our comfort zones. It may involve taking risks, facing fears, and challenging ourselves to grow. But the rewards are immeasurable. When we align our lives with our passions, we create a sense of fulfillment that surpasses any material gains or external validation.

So, dear reader, I encourage you to embark on this journey of self-discovery. Take the time to explore your passions and uncover the unique strengths and talents within you. Embrace the power within and let your passions guide you towards a life filled with meaning and purpose. Remember, the good within you is waiting to be discovered and shared with the world.

Chapter 2: Embracing and Cultivating Your Personal Strengths

Accepting and Celebrating Your Strengths

In the journey of self-discovery, it is crucial to recognize and embrace your unique strengths. We all possess a multitude of talents and capabilities that make us exceptional. However, it is not uncommon for individuals to struggle with accepting and celebrating their own strengths. This subchapter aims to guide you towards finding the good within yourself and appreciating the incredible abilities you bring to the world.

Accepting your strengths is the first step towards self-empowerment. Often, we are our harshest critics, focusing on our weaknesses rather than acknowledging our strengths. Embracing your strengths means recognizing the qualities that set you apart from others, the qualities that make you shine. It is essential to remember that no strength is too small or insignificant. Every talent, every skill, contributes to the beautiful mosaic of your character.

To begin this self-acceptance journey, take the time to reflect on your past achievements. Acknowledge the challenges you have overcome and the skills you have utilized to triumph. Whether it be your ability to communicate effectively, your problem-solving skills, or your creativity, each strength deserves recognition. Celebrate your accomplishments, no matter how big or small, and give yourself credit for the qualities that have brought you success.

It is equally important to celebrate the strengths of others. By embracing and appreciating the strengths of those around us, we create a positive and supportive environment. Recognize that everyone possesses different strengths, and that diversity is what makes the world a vibrant and exciting place. Learning from others and celebrating their unique abilities will not only foster personal growth but also strengthen relationships and build a sense of community.

Remember, accepting and celebrating your strengths does not mean dismissing your weaknesses. It is about finding a balance and understanding that both strengths and weaknesses contribute to personal growth. By acknowledging your strengths, you gain confidence and motivation to continue developing your skills. Simultaneously, recognizing your weaknesses allows you to seek growth opportunities and expand your capabilities.

In conclusion, accepting and celebrating your strengths is a transformative process that leads to self-empowerment and personal growth. By recognizing and appreciating the qualities that make you exceptional, you will develop a stronger sense of self-worth. Embrace your strengths, celebrate the strengths of others, and remember that every talent, no matter how small, has the power to ignite your passions and make a positive impact on the world.

Embracing Your Unique Qualities

In a world that often emphasizes conformity and fitting in, it can be easy to overlook the incredible power that lies within our unique qualities. However, it is these very qualities that make us who we are and set us apart from others. In this subchapter, we will explore the importance of embracing your unique qualities and how doing so can help you find the good within yourself.

Every one of us possesses a set of unique qualities that make us special and valuable. These qualities can range from our talents and skills to our personality traits and experiences. They are the building blocks of our individuality, and when embraced, they can become the catalyst for personal growth and transformation.

Embracing your unique qualities starts with self-acceptance. It is about recognizing and appreciating your strengths, passions, and quirks without judgment or comparison to others. By acknowledging and accepting yourself for who you are, you create a solid foundation for personal development and self-improvement.

When we embrace our unique qualities, we unlock our full potential. Rather than trying to conform to societal expectations or imitate others, we can tap into our natural talents and passions. This allows us to fully express ourselves and cultivate a sense of fulfillment and joy in our lives.

Furthermore, embracing your unique qualities enables you to make a positive impact on the world around you. By embracing and owning your strengths, you can inspire others to do the same. Your unique qualities can become a source of inspiration for those who may be struggling to find their own identity or purpose.

It's important to remember that embracing your unique qualities doesn't mean you are perfect or without flaws. It simply means that you recognize and celebrate the things that make you different. Embracing your unique qualities is a journey of self-discovery and self-acceptance, and it requires patience, self-compassion, and an open mind.

In conclusion, embracing your unique qualities is a powerful and transformative process that can lead to personal growth, fulfillment, and a positive impact on others. By accepting and celebrating your strengths, talents, and quirks, you can unlock your full potential and find the good within yourself. Remember, you are an individual with a unique set of qualities that no one else possesses. Embrace them, nurture them, and let them guide you on your journey towards self-discovery and personal empowerment.

Overcoming Self-Doubt and Comparison

In today's fast-paced and highly competitive world, it is all too easy to fall into the trap of self-doubt and comparison. The constant pressure to achieve and succeed often leads us to question our abilities and worth. However, the key to unlocking our true potential lies in embracing our personal strengths and igniting our passions. In this subchapter, we will explore the strategies and mindset shifts necessary to overcome self-doubt and comparison, allowing us to find and celebrate the good within ourselves.

One of the first steps in overcoming self-doubt is recognizing that we all have unique strengths and talents that make us special. Instead of focusing on what we lack or what others have, we must shift our attention to our own abilities and accomplishments. By acknowledging and appreciating our strengths, we can build a strong foundation of self-confidence.

Comparison, on the other hand, is a toxic habit that robs us of joy and hinders our personal growth. It is crucial to understand that everyone's journey is different, and success can be measured in various ways. Rather than comparing ourselves to others, we should focus on our own progress and milestones. This shift in perspective allows us to celebrate our achievements, big or small, and find fulfillment in our own unique path.

Another effective strategy for overcoming self-doubt and comparison is practicing self-compassion. We are often our harshest critics, but by treating ourselves with kindness and understanding, we can break free from the cycle of negativity. Embracing self-compassion means accepting that we are human and bound to make mistakes. Instead of dwelling on our shortcomings, we can learn from them and use them as stepping stones towards personal growth.

Furthermore, surrounding ourselves with a supportive community can greatly aid in overcoming self-doubt. Connecting with like-minded individuals who uplift and inspire us can provide the encouragement and motivation we need to push past our insecurities. Sharing our struggles and triumphs with others who understand can create a sense of belonging and empowerment.

In conclusion, the journey towards overcoming self-doubt and comparison begins with recognizing and appreciating our unique strengths and accomplishments. By shifting our focus inward and practicing self-compassion, we can break free from the debilitating cycle of negativity. Surrounding ourselves with a supportive community further reinforces our belief in ourselves and our abilities. Let us embrace the power within us, celebrate our individuality, and ignite our passions, for it is through these actions that we will find the true good within ourselves and unlock our fullest potential.

Gratitude for Your Strengths

In a world that often urges us to focus on our flaws and shortcomings, it is easy to overlook the incredible power and potential that resides within each and every one of us. We are constantly bombarded with messages telling us what we should be, how we should look, and what we should strive for, leaving us feeling inadequate and unworthy. However, it is important to remember that true strength lies in embracing who we are and appreciating the unique gifts and talents we possess.

Gratitude for your strengths is not just about acknowledging your accomplishments or comparing yourself to others. It is about recognizing the inherent goodness and value that you bring to the world simply by being yourself. Each of us has a set of strengths that are entirely our own, and it is these strengths that allow us to make a positive impact on those around us.

Finding good in yourself starts with self-reflection and self-awareness. Take the time to explore your passions, interests, and talents. What activities make you feel alive and energized? What tasks do you excel at effortlessly? These are clues to your strengths. Embrace them with gratitude and recognize that they are what make you unique and special.

It is also important to remember that strengths come in many different forms. They can be intellectual, physical, emotional, or even spiritual. Some of us may possess great creativity and imagination, while others may have a knack for problem-solving or leadership. Whatever your strengths may be, they are worth celebrating and nurturing.

Gratitude for your strengths extends beyond just recognizing them. It involves leveraging them to create a fulfilling and purpose-driven life. By utilizing your strengths, you can not only find greater happiness and fulfillment but also make a significant impact in the lives of others. Your strengths are not just for your benefit alone; they are meant to be shared with the world.

So, take a moment to appreciate all that you are and all that you can become. Embrace your strengths with gratitude, for they are the building blocks to unlocking your true potential. Remember, you are a unique individual with a set of strengths that no one else possesses. By finding good in yourself, you can inspire others to do the same and create a ripple effect of positivity and empowerment.

In the journey of self-discovery, let gratitude for your strengths guide you towards embracing your personal power and igniting your passions. You have the power within you to achieve greatness and make a difference. Embrace it, celebrate it, and let your strengths shine brightly for all to see.

Developing and Expanding Your Strengths

In a world that often focuses on our weaknesses and shortcomings, it is crucial to recognize and embrace our personal strengths. Each and every one of us possesses unique talents and abilities that can be tapped into, developed, and expanded upon. By embracing our strengths, we can unlock our full potential and ignite our passions in life.

Finding the good within ourselves is not always an easy task. Society often encourages us to compare ourselves to others, making it easy to overlook our own strengths. However, it is essential to remember that we are all individuals with our own set of skills and qualities that make us exceptional.

To begin the journey of developing and expanding your strengths, it is important to first identify them. Take some time for self-reflection and consider what activities or tasks come naturally to you. What do you excel at? What brings you joy and fulfillment? These are all clues to your personal strengths.

Once you have identified your strengths, it is time to invest in their development. Seek out opportunities to enhance your skills and knowledge in these areas. This could involve taking courses, attending workshops, or even finding a mentor who can guide you in honing your strengths. By actively investing in your strengths, you can build a solid foundation for personal growth and success.

Expanding upon your strengths involves pushing yourself beyond your comfort zone. Challenge yourself to explore new avenues and take on projects that require the utilization of your strengths. This will not only help you grow but also enable you to discover new aspects of your abilities that you may not have realized before.

It is important to remember that developing and expanding your strengths is a continuous process. As you grow and evolve, so too will your strengths. Embrace change and be open to adapting your skills to new challenges and opportunities that come your way.

By recognizing, developing, and expanding upon your strengths, you can unlock the power within yourself. Embracing your personal strengths will not only lead to personal fulfillment but also enable you to make a positive impact on the world around you. So, take the time to discover the good within you, invest in your strengths, and watch as your passions ignite and propel you towards a life of meaning and purpose.

Setting Goals to Enhance Your Strengths

In our journey towards personal growth and self-discovery, it is essential to recognize and embrace our strengths. Each one of us possesses unique qualities and talents that, when harnessed effectively, can lead us towards a more fulfilling and purposeful life. To unlock the power within us, we must learn to set goals that align with our strengths and passions.

Setting goals is not merely a task to be checked off a to-do list; it is a transformative process that empowers us to reach our full potential. When we focus on enhancing our strengths, we become more self-aware, confident, and inspired to take action. It is through setting goals that we can truly tap into our inner potential and channel it towards achieving extraordinary results.

To begin this journey, take a moment to reflect on your strengths and the areas in which you excel. Perhaps you have a natural talent for problem-solving, a creative flair, or exceptional communication skills. Identifying these strengths is the first step towards setting goals that align with who you are and what you are capable of. Embrace these strengths, for they are the key to unlocking your true potential.

Once you have identified your strengths, it is time to set goals that will enhance and magnify them. Start by envisioning what success looks like for you. What would you like to achieve in your personal and professional life? What impact do you want to have on the world around you? Allow your passions and strengths to guide your goal-setting process, ensuring that each goal is in alignment with who you are and what brings you joy.

Remember that setting goals is a dynamic process, and it is essential to regularly evaluate and adjust them as needed. Stay committed to your goals, break them down into manageable steps, and celebrate each milestone along the way. By setting goals that enhance your strengths, you will not only discover the immense power within you but also inspire others to embrace their own strengths and ignite their passions.

In conclusion, setting goals to enhance your strengths is a transformative process that empowers you to reach your full potential. By identifying and embracing your unique qualities and talents, you can set goals that align with who you are and what brings you joy. Stay committed, adjust as needed, and celebrate each milestone along the way. Embrace the power within you and inspire others to do the same.

Seeking Opportunities for Growth

In our journey towards self-discovery, it is essential to recognize the importance of seeking opportunities for growth. Each one of us possesses unique strengths and passions that can be nurtured and developed further. By actively searching for opportunities to grow, we can unlock our full potential and create a fulfilling and purposeful life.

Finding the good within ourselves is an integral part of this process. Often, we focus on our weaknesses, allowing them to overshadow our strengths. However, by shifting our perspective and embracing our personal strengths, we can unlock a world of possibilities. Recognizing our strengths allows us to tap into our natural talents and abilities, enabling us to excel in various aspects of life.

The first step in seeking opportunities for growth is self-reflection. Take the time to explore your passions, interests, and values. Ask yourself what truly brings you joy and fulfillment. By understanding yourself better, you can align your actions with your authentic self, paving the way for personal growth and success.

Additionally, it is crucial to step out of your comfort zone. Growth rarely occurs within the boundaries of familiarity. Embrace challenges and new experiences that push you beyond your limits. This may involve taking on new responsibilities at work, pursuing a new hobby, or even traveling to unfamiliar places. By stepping outside your comfort zone, you open yourself up to new perspectives and opportunities for personal growth.

Furthermore, seeking opportunities for growth involves continuous learning. Embrace a mindset of curiosity and a thirst for knowledge.

Engage in activities that expand your knowledge and skills, such as reading books, attending workshops, or enrolling in courses. Continuous learning not only enhances your personal growth but also equips you with valuable tools to navigate through life's challenges.

Lastly, surround yourself with a supportive network. Seek out individuals who inspire and motivate you to be the best version of yourself. Surrounding yourself with positive influences and mentors can provide guidance and support throughout your personal growth journey.

In conclusion, seeking opportunities for growth is a lifelong process that requires self-reflection, stepping out of your comfort zone, continuous learning, and a supportive network. By embracing your personal strengths and igniting your passions, you can unlock your full potential and create a life filled with purpose and fulfillment. Remember, within each one of us lies the power to achieve greatness – it is up to us to seek the opportunities for growth and unleash our true potential.

Building a Supportive Network

In our journey through life, it is essential to surround ourselves with a supportive network of individuals who uplift and empower us. This subchapter explores the significance of building such a network and how it can help us discover the good within ourselves.

We all possess unique strengths and talents that are waiting to be unleashed. However, it is not always easy to recognize and embrace these personal attributes, especially when faced with self-doubt or negative influences. This is where a supportive network becomes invaluable.

When we surround ourselves with individuals who believe in us and our potential, they provide encouragement, motivation, and guidance. Their unwavering support helps us see the good within ourselves, even when we may struggle to acknowledge it. Through their uplifting words and actions, they help us build the confidence needed to embrace our personal strengths.

A supportive network also acts as a mirror, reflecting our positive qualities back to us. Often, we are our own worst critics, focusing on our flaws rather than celebrating our achievements. However, when surrounded by people who genuinely appreciate and recognize our strengths, we start to view ourselves through a different lens. Their validation reinforces our belief in our abilities and helps us uncover the good that resides within us.

Moreover, a supportive network provides a safe space for personal growth and exploration. It becomes a platform where we can openly share our passions, aspirations, and dreams. Through constructive feedback and guidance, these individuals challenge us to step out of our comfort zones and pursue our goals. They remind us of our potential and inspire us to push beyond our limits, enabling us to discover new dimensions of the good that exists within us.

Building a supportive network is not just about surrounding ourselves with positive influences; it is also about reciprocating that support to others. By being part of a supportive network, we learn the art of giving back and helping others discover the good within themselves. As we uplift and inspire others, we find that our own personal strengths and passions are further ignited.

In conclusion, building a supportive network is a vital aspect of uncovering the good within ourselves. It empowers us, nurtures our self-belief, and provides a platform for personal growth. By surrounding ourselves with individuals who believe in us, we can embrace our strengths and passions, igniting a fire within us that propels us towards success and fulfillment. So, let us cultivate a network of supportive individuals who will help us unlock our true potential and celebrate the goodness that resides within each and every one of us.

Chapter 3: Nurturing Your Passions

Making Time for Your Passions

In our fast-paced and hectic world, finding time for our passions can often seem like a luxury we simply cannot afford. We get caught up in the daily grind, juggling work, family, and other responsibilities, leaving little room for self-discovery and personal growth. However, it is crucial to recognize the immense value that making time for our passions can bring to our lives.

The first step in making time for your passions is to acknowledge the importance of self-care and self-discovery. Many of us get so caught up in meeting the needs of others that we neglect our own desires and aspirations. By making time for our passions, we not only fulfill our own needs but also become more fulfilled individuals, which positively impacts our relationships and overall well-being.

Finding good within oneself is a journey that requires self-reflection and exploration. When we engage in activities that ignite our passions, we tap into our inner strengths and unlock our full potential. It is through these pursuits that we discover our unique talents, interests, and what truly makes us happy. By dedicating time to our passions, we are investing in our personal growth and overall happiness.

While it may seem daunting to carve out time for our passions, it is crucial to prioritize and create a balance in our lives. Start by evaluating your schedule and identifying areas where you can make adjustments. It may mean waking up earlier, cutting back on certain activities, or even delegating tasks to others. Remember, making time for your passions is not selfish; it is an essential part of self-care and personal development.

Once you have identified the time, it is important to set specific goals and create a plan of action. Break down your passions into smaller, manageable tasks and allocate time for them in your schedule. Treat your passion as you would any other commitment, honoring the time you set aside for it. Whether it is painting, writing, playing an instrument, or any other pursuit, consistency is key.

Making time for your passions is not just about finding moments of joy and fulfillment; it is about embracing your personal strengths and igniting your inner fire. By investing in yourself and dedicating time to your passions, you will not only find greater happiness but also inspire and positively impact those around you. Remember, you deserve to pursue what makes you come alive – so make time for your passions and let your inner power shine.

Prioritizing Your Interests

In today's fast-paced world, it can be easy to lose sight of what truly matters to us. We often get caught up in the demands of our daily lives, leaving little time for self-reflection and pursuing our passions. However, it is crucial to prioritize our interests and embrace the power within us. This subchapter aims to guide you on a journey of self-discovery, helping you find the good in yourself and igniting your passions.

The first step in prioritizing your interests is to take a moment to reflect on what truly brings you joy and fulfillment. Ask yourself, "What activities make me lose track of time? What makes me feel alive and inspired?" These questions will help you identify your true passions and interests.

Once you have identified your interests, it is important to make them a priority in your life. This may require making some adjustments to your schedule or setting aside specific time each week to dedicate to your passions. Remember, your interests are not just hobbies; they are an essential part of who you are. By prioritizing them, you are investing in your own personal growth and happiness.

It can be easy to let other responsibilities take precedence over your interests, but it is important to remember that you deserve to pursue what brings you joy. Don't let guilt or societal expectations hold you back. Embrace the power within you and follow your passions with unwavering determination.

In addition to prioritizing your interests, it is crucial to surround yourself with a supportive network of like-minded individuals. Seek out communities or groups that share your interests, as they can provide valuable encouragement, inspiration, and opportunities for collaboration. By connecting with others who share your passions, you can fuel your own personal growth and find even greater fulfillment in your pursuits.

Prioritizing your interests is not a selfish act; rather, it is an act of self-care and self-discovery. By embracing your personal strengths and igniting your passions, you are not only enriching your own life but also inspiring those around you to do the same. So, take the time to prioritize your interests, find the good within you, and let your passions guide you towards a life of purpose and fulfillment.

Incorporating Passion into Your Daily Life

Passion is a powerful force that resides within each and every one of us. It is the driving energy that propels us towards our goals, ignites our creativity, and brings fulfillment to our lives. However, many people struggle to incorporate their passions into their daily routines, often letting the demands of life overshadow their true desires. If you find yourself in this situation, fear not! This subchapter is dedicated to helping you discover ways to infuse your passions into your everyday life, allowing you to find the good in yourself and live a more fulfilling existence.

The key to incorporating passion into your daily life lies in intentionality and prioritization. Start by identifying your passions – those activities, interests, and pursuits that truly light a fire within you. It could be anything, from playing a musical instrument to cooking, writing, or even gardening. Once you have identified your passions, it is crucial to make them a priority in your daily routine. Set aside dedicated time each day to engage in these activities, even if it is just for a few minutes. By doing so, you are honoring your true self and nurturing your inner flame.

Another way to incorporate passion into your daily life is by seeking out opportunities that align with your interests. Look for ways to integrate your passions into your work, hobbies, or even volunteering activities. For instance, if you have a passion for writing, consider starting a blog or contributing articles to online platforms. If you love working with animals, explore volunteer opportunities at local shelters. By actively seeking out avenues that allow you to engage with your passions, you are creating a life that is more aligned with your true self.

Furthermore, it is important to surround yourself with like-minded individuals who share your passions or support your journey. Seek out communities, whether online or offline, that provide a space for you to connect with others who understand and appreciate your interests. Engaging with these communities can provide inspiration, encouragement, and even collaboration opportunities, further fueling your passion and helping you to discover the good within yourself.

Incorporating passion into your daily life is not always easy, but it is undoubtedly worth the effort. By intentionally prioritizing your passions, seeking out opportunities that align with your interests, and surrounding yourself with like-minded individuals, you can create a life that is filled with purpose and fulfillment. Embrace your personal strengths, ignite your passions, and let the power within you shine bright!

Balancing Responsibilities and Pursuits

In today's fast-paced world, it is easy to get caught up in the whirlwind of responsibilities and forget about our passions and personal strengths. We often find ourselves juggling work, family, relationships, and countless other obligations, leaving little time for self-reflection and personal growth. However, it is crucial to find a balance between our responsibilities and pursuits, as this is where true fulfillment lies.

The subchapter "Balancing Responsibilities and Pursuits" in the book "The Power Within: Embracing Personal Strengths and Igniting Your Passions" aims to guide readers towards finding the good within themselves amidst the chaos of everyday life.

First and foremost, it is essential to identify and embrace your personal strengths. Each one of us possesses unique qualities that make us special. By recognizing and nurturing these strengths, we can tap into our full potential and achieve a sense of self-fulfillment. This subchapter explores various techniques and exercises to help readers uncover their strengths and leverage them in their personal and professional lives.

Additionally, the subchapter emphasizes the importance of setting boundaries and prioritizing your pursuits. It is easy to become overwhelmed by numerous responsibilities, but by learning to say no when necessary and setting realistic expectations, you can create more time and space for your passions. This section provides practical tips on time management and effective goal setting, helping readers strike a balance between their obligations and personal desires.

Furthermore, the subchapter delves into the concept of self-care. It highlights the significance of taking care of oneself physically, mentally, and emotionally, as neglecting self-care can lead to burnout and unhappiness. Readers will explore various self-care practices and learn how to incorporate them into their daily routines, ensuring that they are not only meeting their responsibilities but also nourishing their own well-being.

Ultimately, "Balancing Responsibilities and Pursuits" is a powerful reminder that finding the good within ourselves and pursuing our passions should not be neglected amidst our busy lives. By embracing our personal strengths, setting boundaries, and prioritizing self-care, we can achieve a sense of harmony and fulfillment. This subchapter serves as a valuable resource for anyone seeking to strike a balance between their responsibilities and pursuits, offering guidance and inspiration to uncover the power within.

Fueling Your Passions

We all possess unique strengths and talents that define who we are as individuals. However, discovering and embracing these personal strengths can sometimes be a challenge. In today's fast-paced world, it is crucial to take the time to explore our passions and find the good within ourselves.

"Fueling Your Passions" is a subchapter in the compelling book, "The Power Within: Embracing Personal Strengths and Igniting Your Passions." This chapter is dedicated to helping every individual unleash their potential and find joy in pursuing their passions.

The journey of self-discovery begins with understanding ourselves on a deeper level. It is essential to identify our natural talents, interests, and values. By recognizing what truly resonates with us, we can align our passions with our goals and aspirations. This alignment creates a powerful force that propels us forward towards success and fulfillment.

In "Fueling Your Passions," you will embark on a transformative journey that encourages self-reflection and introspection. Through thought-provoking exercises and practical tips, you will gain insight into your unique strengths and talents. This newfound self-awareness will enable you to channel your passions into meaningful action.

The subchapter also delves into the importance of cultivating a positive mindset. Often, we tend to focus on our weaknesses and shortcomings, overlooking the incredible strengths we possess. By shifting our perspective and embracing a positive outlook, we can tap into our inner potential and unlock the doors to endless possibilities.

Discovering and nurturing our passions not only brings us personal fulfillment but also benefits those around us. When we are passionate about something, it radiates positive energy that inspires and motivates others. Our passions can serve as a catalyst for change, allowing us to make a significant impact on the world.

No matter where you are in life, "Fueling Your Passions" is a chapter that will resonate with everyone. Whether you are a student seeking direction, a professional yearning for a more fulfilling career, or someone who wants to reignite their zest for life, this subchapter will guide you towards finding the good within yourself.

"The Power Within: Embracing Personal Strengths and Igniting Your Passions" is a powerful tool that empowers individuals from all walks of life. Through its insightful guidance and practical wisdom, it encourages you to embrace your unique strengths, reignite your passions, and unlock the extraordinary potential within you. So, embark on this remarkable journey of self-discovery and unleash the power within you.

Learning and Gaining Knowledge

In a world that constantly bombards us with information and distractions, it is essential to understand the true power of learning and gaining knowledge. Whether you are a student striving for success in your academics, a young professional looking to advance in your career, or someone simply seeking personal growth and self-improvement, the ability to learn and acquire knowledge is a vital tool in your journey towards finding the good within yourself.

Learning is not just about acquiring facts and figures; it is about expanding our minds, broadening our horizons, and opening ourselves up to new possibilities. It is a lifelong process that should be embraced by everyone, regardless of age or background. Learning allows us to challenge our preconceived notions, question our beliefs, and develop a deeper understanding of the world around us.

Gaining knowledge goes hand in hand with learning, as it empowers us to make informed decisions and explore our passions. Knowledge gives us the confidence to pursue our dreams, to take risks, and to overcome obstacles. When we have a solid foundation of knowledge, we can navigate through life with a sense of purpose and direction.

However, it is important to recognize that knowledge is not limited to traditional academic settings. Learning can occur in various forms, such as reading books, attending workshops, engaging in meaningful conversations, or even through personal experiences. The key is to remain curious and open-minded, always seeking opportunities to expand our knowledge and understanding.

In the pursuit of finding the good within ourselves, learning and gaining knowledge are invaluable. They allow us to discover our strengths, identify our passions, and tap into our full potential. By continually learning, we can uncover hidden talents, nurture our creativity, and cultivate a sense of fulfillment and purpose in our lives.

So, let us embrace the power of learning and gaining knowledge. Let us commit to being lifelong learners, constantly seeking new opportunities to grow and evolve. Remember, knowledge is not a destination; it is a journey. And by embarking on this journey, we can truly unleash our personal strengths, ignite our passions, and uncover the limitless power within ourselves.

Seeking Inspiration from Others

In our journey of self-discovery, it is essential to seek inspiration from others. We are all capable of finding the good within ourselves, but sometimes we need a little push to ignite our passions and embrace our personal strengths. The power of seeking inspiration from others lies in the ability to learn from their experiences, gain new perspectives, and draw motivation to unlock our true potential.

One of the most effective ways to find inspiration is by surrounding yourself with individuals who radiate positivity and embody the qualities you admire. Whether it is a friend, family member, mentor, or even a role model you admire from afar, observing their actions and mindset can provide valuable insights. By observing their journey, you can learn how they have embraced their personal strengths, overcome challenges, and ignited their passions. Their stories can serve as a guiding light, showing you that it is possible to find the good within yourself and live a fulfilling life.

Moreover, seeking inspiration from others is not limited to personal connections. Books, biographies, documentaries, and even online platforms can be excellent sources of inspiration. These resources offer a treasure trove of stories and experiences from people who have triumphed over adversity and found the courage to pursue their passions. By immersing yourself in their narratives, you can gain a fresh perspective, discover new ideas, and find inspiration to embark on your own journey of self-discovery.

However, it is important to remember that seeking inspiration from others should not lead to comparison or self-doubt. Each person's journey is unique, and what works for someone else may not necessarily work for you. Instead of comparing yourself to others, focus on extracting the lessons and principles that resonate with your own values and aspirations. Use these insights as building blocks to shape your own path towards self-discovery and personal growth.

Remember, the power to find the good within yourself lies within you, but seeking inspiration from others can be a catalyst on your journey. Embrace the opportunity to learn from those around you, be it through personal connections or the stories of remarkable individuals. Allow their experiences to ignite the fire within you, awakening your passions and empowering you to embrace your personal strengths. By seeking inspiration from others, you can unlock the power within yourself and create a life filled with purpose, meaning, and fulfillment.

Taking Risks and Embracing Challenges

In our journey through life, we are often presented with opportunities that require us to step out of our comfort zones and take risks. These risks and challenges can be intimidating, but they also hold the potential for great personal growth and discovery. In this subchapter, we will explore the importance of taking risks and embracing challenges to unlock the power within ourselves.

Each one of us possesses a unique set of strengths and talents that may remain dormant if we do not push ourselves to try new things. By taking risks, we open ourselves up to a world of possibilities. It is through these risks that we can truly discover the depths of our abilities and uncover our hidden potential. Moreover, taking risks allows us to break free from the limitations we have placed upon ourselves, enabling personal growth and development.

Embracing challenges is another crucial aspect of finding the good within ourselves. Challenges may seem daunting at first, but they provide us with the opportunity to learn and grow. When faced with a challenge, we are forced to tap into our inner strength, creativity, and problem-solving skills. It is during these moments that we learn the most about ourselves and our capabilities. By embracing challenges, we not only develop resilience and perseverance, but we also gain a sense of accomplishment and fulfillment when we overcome them.

Taking risks and embracing challenges also helps us to expand our comfort zones. When we step outside of what is familiar and comfortable, we open ourselves up to new experiences, perspectives, and opportunities. This expansion allows us to develop a greater understanding of ourselves and the world around us. It allows us to break free from the constraints of our comfort zones and to explore new passions and interests.

Ultimately, taking risks and embracing challenges is a powerful tool for personal growth and self-discovery. By pushing ourselves to try new things and face our fears head-on, we unlock the hidden potential within us. We gain confidence in our abilities and learn to trust ourselves. We develop resilience, adaptability, and a zest for life. So, don't be afraid to take risks and embrace challenges, for it is through these actions that we find the good within ourselves and ignite our passions.

Chapter 4: Igniting Your Passions and Achieving Success

Setting Goals Aligned with Your Passions

In the journey of self-discovery, one of the most crucial aspects is setting goals that are aligned with your passions. When you align your goals with your passions, you create a powerful synergy that propels you towards success and fulfillment. It is essential for everyone, regardless of their background or circumstances, to find the good within themselves and harness their personal strengths. This subchapter will guide you on how to set goals that align with your passions and ignite the power within you.

Passions are the driving force behind our actions and the key to unlocking our full potential. They are the things that excite us, make us feel alive, and bring us immense joy. When we align our goals with our passions, we tap into an endless reserve of motivation and determination that propels us forward even in the face of challenges.

The first step towards setting goals aligned with your passions is to identify what truly makes you come alive. Reflect on your interests, hobbies, and the activities that bring you the most satisfaction. Take the time to explore different areas and experiment with new experiences. This self-exploration will help you uncover your true passions and understand what truly resonates with you.

Once you have identified your passions, it is time to set goals that align with them. Start by defining your long-term vision and aspirations. What is it that you ultimately want to achieve? Break down this vision into smaller, actionable goals that can be achieved within a specific timeframe. These smaller goals will serve as milestones on your journey towards your ultimate passion-driven vision.

It is important to ensure that your goals are realistic and achievable. Setting unrealistic goals can lead to frustration and disappointment. Take into consideration your current circumstances, resources, and capabilities when setting your goals. This will enable you to maintain a positive mindset and stay motivated throughout the process.

As you embark on your goal-setting journey, remember to regularly evaluate and reassess your progress. Celebrate your milestones and be open to adapting your goals as needed. Embrace the inevitable challenges and setbacks as opportunities for growth and learning. By aligning your goals with your passions, you will not only find the good within yourself but also unleash a powerful force that can propel you towards a life of fulfillment and success.

In conclusion, setting goals aligned with your passions is a transformative process that can unlock the power within you. By identifying your passions, breaking down your long-term vision, and setting achievable goals, you can tap into an endless well of motivation and determination. Embrace this process, and you will discover the immense potential within you to find the good and embrace your personal strengths.

Defining Clear and Measurable Goals

In our journey towards self-discovery and personal growth, it is crucial to set clear and measurable goals. Goals serve as the roadmap that guides us, helping us stay focused, motivated, and committed to achieving our dreams. In this subchapter, we will explore the importance of defining these goals and how they can help us find the good within ourselves.

Clear goals provide us with direction and purpose. They allow us to identify what we truly want and provide a sense of clarity in our lives. When we have a clear goal in mind, we can concentrate our efforts on the actions that will lead us towards its attainment. Without a clear goal, we may find ourselves wandering aimlessly, unsure of what steps to take next. By defining our goals, we empower ourselves to make informed decisions and take purposeful actions.

Furthermore, setting measurable goals allows us to track our progress effectively. Measurability brings objectivity to our aspirations, enabling us to evaluate whether we are moving in the right direction or need to adjust our strategies. When we can measure our progress, we gain a sense of achievement and are motivated to continue working towards our goals. It also helps us identify any obstacles or setbacks, allowing us to make necessary adjustments and stay on track.

Defining clear and measurable goals not only helps us find the good within ourselves but also enables us to tap into our full potential. When we set goals that align with our passions, strengths, and values, we create a sense of purpose and fulfillment. By focusing on our innate abilities and passions, we can unlock our true potential and unleash our talents. This leads to increased self-confidence, as we begin to recognize the unique gifts and strengths we possess.

As we embrace our personal strengths and ignite our passions, it is crucial to define clear and measurable goals. They provide us with direction, motivation, and a sense of purpose. By setting goals that align with our values and passions, we can tap into our full potential and find the good within ourselves. So, let us take the time to reflect on our aspirations and define clear, measurable goals that will guide us towards personal growth, fulfillment, and a life of purpose.

Creating a Plan of Action

In our journey towards self-discovery and personal growth, it is essential to have a plan of action. Without a clear direction and purpose, we may find ourselves wandering aimlessly, unsure of how to harness our personal strengths and ignite our passions. A plan of action serves as a roadmap, guiding us towards finding the good within ourselves and unlocking our true potential.

The first step in creating a plan of action is to reflect on your personal strengths and passions. Take the time to identify what makes you unique and what brings you joy. What activities or skills do you excel in? What are you truly passionate about? Understanding your strengths and passions will help you to focus your energy and efforts in the right direction.

Once you have a clear understanding of your strengths and passions, it is time to set goals. These goals will serve as the milestones on your journey towards self-discovery and personal growth. Make sure your goals are specific, measurable, achievable, relevant, and time-bound (SMART). This will ensure that your goals are realistic and attainable, giving you a sense of accomplishment as you progress.

Next, break down your goals into actionable steps. By breaking large goals into smaller, manageable tasks, you can avoid feeling overwhelmed and stay motivated. Each step should be clear and concise, with a specific action attached to it. This will help you stay focused and accountable as you work towards achieving your goals.

Remember to celebrate your achievements along the way. Acknowledge the progress you have made, no matter how small.

Celebrating your successes will boost your confidence and provide the motivation to continue moving forward.

Lastly, it is important to regularly review and revise your plan of action. As you grow and evolve, your goals and priorities may change. By regularly evaluating your plan, you can ensure that it remains aligned with your personal strengths and passions.

Creating a plan of action is a powerful tool in finding the good within yourself. It provides clarity, focus, and a sense of purpose. With a plan in place, you can navigate your personal journey with confidence and ignite your passions along the way. So take the time to reflect, set goals, break them down into actionable steps, celebrate your achievements, and regularly review your plan. Embrace your personal strengths, ignite your passions, and unleash the power within you.

Tracking Progress and Making Adjustments

In our journey of self-discovery and personal growth, it is important to not only recognize our strengths and passions but also to constantly evaluate our progress. Tracking our progress allows us to stay motivated, make necessary adjustments, and continue on the path towards becoming the best version of ourselves. This subchapter explores the significance of tracking progress and provides practical tips on how to make effective adjustments along the way.

Tracking progress is like navigating a ship through uncharted waters. Without a compass and a map, we would be lost at sea. Similarly, without monitoring our progress, we may lose sight of our goals and aspirations. Tracking progress helps us understand where we are in our journey, how far we have come, and how much further we need to go. It provides a sense of direction and purpose, giving us the motivation to keep pushing forward.

One effective way to track progress is by setting clear and measurable goals. By breaking down our larger goals into smaller, achievable milestones, we can celebrate our progress along the way. We can use tools such as journals, spreadsheets, or even smartphone apps to record our achievements and track our growth. Reflecting on these milestones not only boosts our self-confidence but also allows us to identify areas where we may need to make adjustments.

Making adjustments is a crucial part of personal growth. Life is dynamic, and circumstances change. What worked for us yesterday may not work for us today. By regularly evaluating our progress, we can identify any obstacles or challenges that may be hindering our growth. Adjustments could range from changing our approach, seeking additional resources or support, or even redefining our goals and passions. Embracing the process of adjustment allows us to adapt, learn, and grow in new and unexpected ways.

It is important to remember that tracking progress and making adjustments is not a linear process. It is a continuous cycle of self-reflection and growth. Along the way, we may encounter setbacks or face periods of stagnation. However, it is during these moments that we must remind ourselves of the good within us. We all have unique strengths and abilities that can help us persevere and overcome any obstacles that come our way.

In conclusion, tracking progress and making adjustments are vital components of our journey towards self-discovery and personal growth. By tracking our progress, we gain clarity, direction, and motivation. Making adjustments allows us to adapt to changing circumstances and continue moving forward. Remember, within each of us lies the power to embrace our personal strengths and ignite our passions. So, let us track our progress, make necessary adjustments, and unleash the power within us to create a life of purpose and fulfillment.

Overcoming Obstacles and Persevering

Introduction:
In life, we all encounter obstacles and face challenges that can sometimes leave us feeling defeated and discouraged. However, it is during these trying times that our true strength and resilience shine through. In this subchapter, titled "Overcoming Obstacles and Persevering," we will explore the power within each and every one of us to face adversity head-on, find the good within ourselves, and embrace our personal strengths to ignite our passions.

Finding Good in You:
Often, when faced with obstacles, we tend to focus on our weaknesses and shortcomings. However, it is crucial to shift our mindset and recognize the innate goodness within ourselves. Each one of us possesses unique qualities and strengths that can help us overcome any hurdle that comes our way. Take a moment to reflect on your past accomplishments and the positive impact you have made on others' lives. By recognizing and embracing these qualities, you will build the self-confidence necessary to tackle any obstacle that stands in your path.

The Power of Perseverance:
Perseverance is the key to overcoming obstacles and achieving success. It is the ability to push forward, even when faced with setbacks and failures. Throughout history, countless individuals have faced tremendous challenges but refused to give up. From Thomas Edison's numerous failed attempts before inventing the light bulb to J.K. Rowling's rejection letters before publishing the Harry Potter series, their stories inspire us to never surrender to adversity. By cultivating a

resilient mindset and understanding that setbacks are merely stepping stones towards success, you will develop the strength to persevere and overcome any obstacle that comes your way.

Harnessing Personal Strengths:
Each one of us possesses a unique set of strengths and talents. These strengths can be harnessed and nurtured to help us overcome obstacles and achieve our goals. Take the time to identify your personal strengths and how they can be utilized to navigate challenges effectively. Whether it is your creativity, problem-solving abilities, or emotional intelligence, embracing and honing these strengths will empower you to face adversity with confidence and determination.

Igniting Your Passions:
Passion is a powerful force that can drive us to overcome even the most daunting obstacles. When we are deeply passionate about something, we become more resilient, determined, and focused. Take the time to identify your passions and align them with your goals. By igniting your passions, you will find the motivation and energy needed to persevere through any obstacle that comes your way.

Conclusion:
In life, overcoming obstacles and persevering is not always easy, but it is essential for personal growth and success. By recognizing the good within ourselves, harnessing our personal strengths, and igniting our passions, we can face any challenge head-on. Remember, you possess the power within to overcome anything that stands in your way. Embrace your personal strengths, cultivate resilience, and let your passions fuel your journey towards a brighter and more fulfilling future.

Dealing with Fear and Failure

Fear and failure are two inevitable aspects of life that can hinder our growth and prevent us from reaching our full potential. However, it is important to understand that these challenges can also serve as catalysts for personal development if we learn to embrace them. In this subchapter, we will explore effective strategies for dealing with fear and failure, allowing you to harness your inner strength and ignite your passions.

Fear is a powerful emotion that can paralyze us and prevent us from taking risks. It is crucial to recognize that fear is a natural response to the unknown and can often be an indication that we are stepping out of our comfort zone. By reframing our perspective, we can view fear as an opportunity for growth rather than a limitation. Embracing fear allows us to conquer it, pushing past our boundaries and discovering the untapped potential within ourselves.

Failure, on the other hand, is often seen as a negative outcome. However, it is important to reframe failure as a learning experience rather than a setback. Every successful individual has faced failure at some point in their journey. It is through these failures that we learn valuable lessons, gain resilience, and develop a deeper understanding of ourselves. By embracing failure, we can transform it into a stepping stone towards success.

To effectively deal with fear and failure, it is essential to cultivate self-compassion. Understand that everyone experiences fear and failure, and it does not diminish your worth or potential. Treat yourself with kindness and forgiveness, allowing room for growth and improvement. By focusing on self-acceptance and positive self-talk, you can build the inner strength necessary to overcome any obstacle.

Additionally, surrounding yourself with a supportive network is crucial. Seek out individuals who inspire and uplift you, encouraging you to pursue your passions despite the fear of failure. Engage in open conversations about fears and failures, sharing experiences and insights. This sense of community can provide the reassurance and motivation needed to overcome challenges.

Ultimately, dealing with fear and failure is a continuous process that requires patience and perseverance. By reframing fear as an opportunity and failure as a stepping stone, you can harness your inner strength and ignite your passions. Embrace the journey of self-discovery, finding the good within yourself and using it as a driving force towards personal growth and success. Remember, you have the power within you to overcome any fear and turn failure into triumph.

Building Resilience and Determination

In our journey through life, we often encounter obstacles and face challenges that can test our resolve and push us to our limits. It is during these tough times that the power of resilience and determination becomes essential. The ability to bounce back from setbacks and stay focused on our goals is what sets successful individuals apart. In this subchapter, we explore the significance of building resilience and determination, and how they can help us uncover the goodness within ourselves.

Resilience is the strength to withstand adversity and come out stronger on the other side. It is the ability to adapt to change, learn from failure, and move forward with newfound wisdom. When we possess resilience, we are able to face life's challenges head-on, embracing them as opportunities for growth. By building resilience, we tap into our inner strength and unleash our full potential.

Determination, on the other hand, is the unwavering resolve to achieve our goals, no matter the obstacles. It is the fuel that keeps us going when the going gets tough. Determination pushes us to take risks, step out of our comfort zones, and persist in the face of adversity. When we possess determination, we become unstoppable, driven by a burning passion to make our dreams a reality.

To build resilience and determination, it is crucial to first recognize and appreciate the goodness within ourselves. Each one of us possesses unique strengths and talents that can help us overcome challenges and reach our full potential. By acknowledging our abilities and focusing on our positive qualities, we can cultivate a mindset of self-belief and confidence.

Additionally, surrounding ourselves with a supportive network of family, friends, and mentors can greatly contribute to our resilience and determination. These individuals can provide guidance, encouragement, and a shoulder to lean on during difficult times. Together, we can share our experiences, learn from one another, and inspire each other to keep pushing forward.

Lastly, embracing failure as a stepping stone to success is crucial in building resilience and determination. Failure is not an indication of weakness but rather an opportunity to learn and grow. By reframing failure as a valuable learning experience, we can bounce back stronger, armed with newfound knowledge and determination to succeed.

In conclusion, building resilience and determination is essential for unleashing the power within ourselves. By recognizing the goodness within us, surrounding ourselves with a supportive network, and embracing failure as a catalyst for growth, we can cultivate resilience and determination that will propel us towards our goals. So let us embark on this journey of self-discovery, and unlock the limitless potential that resides within each and every one of us.

Seeking Support and Encouragement

Subchapter: Seeking Support and Encouragement

Introduction:

In our journey through life, we often face challenges and obstacles that can leave us feeling overwhelmed and doubtful about our abilities. During such times, seeking support and encouragement becomes crucial to help us navigate through the rough patches and rediscover our inner strength. This subchapter aims to guide you on the path of finding the good within yourself, while also harnessing the power of support and encouragement from others.

Unleashing Your Strengths:

To find the good within yourself, it is essential to tap into your personal strengths. Take a moment to reflect on the unique qualities and talents that make you who you are. Embrace these strengths and let them guide you towards your passions and goals. Remember, every individual possesses a set of strengths that can be honed and utilized to overcome challenges.

Recognizing the Importance of Self-Encouragement:

While seeking support from others is important, self-encouragement plays a vital role in your personal growth. Cultivate positive self-talk and affirmations to boost your confidence and motivate yourself during difficult times. By acknowledging your accomplishments, however small they may seem, you will develop a resilient mindset, enabling you to face any adversity with determination.

The Power of Support:

Seeking support from others is not a sign of weakness but a testament to your strength and willingness to grow. Surround yourself with individuals who believe in your abilities and aspirations. They will provide the encouragement and motivation needed to keep moving forward. Share your dreams, fears, and challenges with trusted friends, family, or mentors who can offer guidance, empathy, and support.

Finding Supportive Communities:

It is equally important to seek out supportive communities that align with your interests and passions. Joining groups, clubs, or organizations that share your values and goals can provide a network of individuals who understand and encourage your journey. Engaging with like-minded people will not only offer valuable support but also open doors to new opportunities and collaborations.

In conclusion, seeking support and encouragement is an essential aspect of embracing your personal strengths and igniting your passions. By recognizing the good within yourself and reaching out for support, you will embark on a transformative journey towards personal growth and fulfillment. Remember, you are not alone in your quest, and there are always individuals and communities ready to offer the guidance and encouragement you need.

Chapter 5: Living a Fulfilling Life through Personal Strengths and Passions

Embracing Growth and Continuous Learning

In today's fast-paced world, it is essential to embrace growth and continuous learning in order to thrive. This subchapter is dedicated to helping every individual discover the power within themselves by finding the good in them and igniting their passions.

The journey towards personal growth starts with self-reflection. Taking the time to understand your strengths, weaknesses, and passions is crucial. By identifying your unique qualities and talents, you can harness them to achieve success and fulfillment in all areas of life. Remember, everyone has something special within them, waiting to be discovered.

Once you have identified your strengths, it is important to embrace them wholeheartedly. Too often, we underestimate our own abilities and limit our potential. Embracing your strengths means acknowledging them, nurturing them, and utilizing them to their fullest extent. This not only leads to personal growth but also allows you to make a positive impact on the world around you.

However, personal growth is not a one-time achievement; it is a lifelong journey. Continuous learning plays a vital role in this process. Cultivating a growth mindset, which views challenges as opportunities for growth, allows you to embrace new experiences and expand your knowledge and skills. Whether it's through formal education, reading, attending workshops, or seeking mentorship, there are countless ways to continue learning and evolving.

Embracing growth and continuous learning also requires stepping out of your comfort zone. It is natural to feel hesitant or fearful when faced with new challenges, but growth happens when you push beyond your limitations. Take risks, try new things, and embrace failure as a valuable learning experience. Each setback is an opportunity to learn, grow, and become a better version of yourself.

Remember, personal growth and continuous learning are not just about achieving external success. It is about cultivating a deep sense of self-awareness, finding joy in the journey, and living a life aligned with your passions and values. By embracing growth and continuous learning, you open yourself up to a world of possibilities and unlock the power within you.

So, start today. Embrace your strengths, nurture your passions, and commit to a lifetime of growth and learning. You have everything you need within you to create a life of purpose, fulfillment, and success. Embrace the power within and let it guide you towards a brighter future.

Cultivating a Growth Mindset

In a world that often focuses on our weaknesses and shortcomings, it is crucial to embrace a growth mindset and discover the power within ourselves. This subchapter aims to guide every individual towards finding the good within themselves and igniting their passions.

A growth mindset is the belief that our talents, abilities, and intelligence can be developed through dedication, hard work, and perseverance. Unlike a fixed mindset, which believes that our qualities are fixed traits that cannot be changed, a growth mindset opens up a world of possibilities and personal growth.

The first step in cultivating a growth mindset is to acknowledge and appreciate your unique strengths and abilities. Each one of us possesses a set of skills and talents that make us exceptional. Take the time to reflect on your past achievements, accomplishments, and positive experiences. By recognizing and celebrating your successes, you will build confidence in your abilities and lay the foundation for personal growth.

Next, it is important to embrace challenges and view them as opportunities for growth. Instead of shying away from difficult tasks or uncertain situations, approach them with a positive mindset. Understand that setbacks and failures are not indicators of incompetence but rather stepping stones towards improvement. By reframing challenges as opportunities to learn and develop new skills, you will develop resilience and become more open to pursuing your passions.

Another key aspect of cultivating a growth mindset is seeking out feedback and learning from others. Embrace constructive criticism as a valuable tool for growth rather than a personal attack. Surround yourself with individuals who support your personal development and are willing to provide honest feedback. By actively seeking out different perspectives, you will broaden your horizons and gain new insights into your strengths and areas for improvement.

Lastly, never underestimate the power of perseverance and a positive attitude. Cultivating a growth mindset requires dedication and a willingness to push beyond comfort zones. Embrace failures as learning opportunities and remain optimistic in the face of adversity. By adopting a positive mindset and persisting in your efforts, you will continue to grow and unleash your full potential.

In conclusion, cultivating a growth mindset is essential for finding the good within yourself and igniting your passions. By acknowledging your strengths, embracing challenges, seeking feedback, and persevering with a positive attitude, you will unlock your personal strengths and embrace the power within. Remember, personal growth is a journey, and with a growth mindset, the possibilities are endless.

Embracing New Opportunities and Challenges

In life, we are constantly presented with new opportunities and challenges that can shape the course of our journey. These moments allow us to grow, evolve, and discover the incredible potential that lies within each one of us. In this subchapter, we will explore the importance of embracing these new opportunities and challenges as a means of finding the good within ourselves.

The first step in embracing new opportunities and challenges is to adopt a mindset of curiosity and open-mindedness. Instead of shying away from the unknown, we must approach it with enthusiasm and a willingness to learn. By doing so, we allow ourselves to tap into our personal strengths and ignite our passions. Remember, it is through these experiences that we truly discover what we are capable of achieving.

As we navigate through life, we often encounter challenges that may seem insurmountable at first. However, it is crucial to recognize that these obstacles are not roadblocks but rather opportunities for growth. By reframing our perspective, we can view challenges as stepping stones to success rather than barriers to our progress. This mindset shift allows us to develop resilience, determination, and a sense of self-belief that propels us forward in the face of adversity.

Embracing new opportunities and challenges also requires us to step outside of our comfort zones. It is only by venturing into the unknown that we can truly discover our hidden talents and passions. This may involve taking risks, trying new things, or pursuing unfamiliar paths.

While it may be intimidating, remember that growth and self-discovery lie just beyond the boundaries of our comfort zones.

Furthermore, embracing new opportunities and challenges allows us to unleash our creativity. When faced with unfamiliar situations, we are forced to think outside the box and explore innovative solutions. This not only enhances our problem-solving skills but also nurtures our ability to adapt and thrive in an ever-changing world.

In conclusion, embracing new opportunities and challenges is essential for finding the good within ourselves. By adopting a mindset of curiosity, reframing challenges, stepping outside of our comfort zones, and unleashing our creativity, we unlock our personal strengths and ignite our passions. Remember, the power to embrace these opportunities lies within each one of us. So, let us embark on this journey of self-discovery, growth, and fulfillment, embracing the endless possibilities that await us.

Seeking Feedback for Improvement

In our journey towards self-discovery and personal growth, one crucial aspect often overlooked is seeking feedback from others. Feedback serves as a powerful tool for understanding our strengths, weaknesses, and areas for improvement. It allows us to gain valuable insights into our actions, behaviors, and the impact we have on those around us. By actively seeking feedback, we can unlock our true potential and ignite our passions.

Feedback is not something to be feared or avoided; instead, it should be embraced as an opportunity for growth. It is through feedback that we can uncover aspects of ourselves that we may have overlooked or underestimated. By seeking feedback, we open ourselves up to a wealth of knowledge and perspectives that can help us find the good within ourselves.

When seeking feedback, it is important to approach it with an open mind and a willingness to learn. Being receptive to feedback requires humility and a genuine desire to improve. Embracing feedback means understanding that we are not perfect and that there is always room for growth and development. It is a courageous step towards becoming the best version of ourselves.

Feedback can come from various sources, such as friends, family, colleagues, mentors, or even strangers. Each person brings a unique perspective and can offer valuable insights. However, it is crucial to choose reliable sources who have our best interests at heart and who can provide constructive criticism rather than destructive judgment.

To seek feedback effectively, it is essential to create a safe and open environment where people feel comfortable sharing their thoughts. Encourage others to be honest and transparent, and assure them that their feedback will be taken seriously. Actively listen to their opinions, ask clarifying questions, and reflect on their feedback without becoming defensive. Remember, feedback is not a personal attack but an opportunity to grow and improve.

Once we have received feedback, it is crucial to take the time to reflect upon it. Consider the validity of the feedback, identifying any recurring themes or patterns. Evaluate how the feedback aligns with your own self-perception and values. Then, use this newfound knowledge to set goals and develop an action plan for improvement.

In conclusion, seeking feedback is a vital step in finding the good within ourselves. It allows us to gain valuable insights, discover our blind spots, and make positive changes in our lives. By embracing feedback, we can harness our personal strengths, ignite our passions, and unlock the power within us. So, let us embrace the opportunity to seek feedback and embrace personal growth, for it is through this process that we can truly become the best versions of ourselves.

Inspiring Others through Your Journey

In our journey through life, we often discover that we possess immense power within ourselves. The power to overcome obstacles, achieve our goals, and make a positive impact on those around us. This power comes from embracing our personal strengths and igniting our passions. By doing so, we not only find the good within ourselves but also have the ability to inspire others along the way.

Each one of us has a unique story to tell, filled with experiences that have shaped us into the individuals we are today. When we share our journey with others, we open the door for inspiration and connection. By being vulnerable and showing our authentic selves, we allow others to see the strength and courage that resides within us. This, in turn, encourages them to explore their own strengths and passions.

Inspiration is contagious. When we live our lives passionately, pursuing our dreams and goals, we become a beacon of light for those around us. People are drawn to individuals who radiate positivity and determination. By embracing our personal strengths, we not only find fulfillment within ourselves but also inspire others to do the same.

It is important to remember that our journey is not always smooth sailing. We face challenges, setbacks, and moments of self-doubt. However, it is during these times that our true strength shines through. By sharing our struggles and how we overcame them, we show others the power of perseverance and resilience. We become living proof that no matter how difficult life may seem, there is always a way forward.

Inspirational journeys come in all shapes and sizes. Whether you have triumphed over adversity, pursued a passion against all odds, or simply discovered the power of self-belief, your story has the potential to inspire someone else. By sharing your experiences, you give others the hope and motivation they need to embark on their own journey of self-discovery.

So, embrace your personal strengths, ignite your passions, and let your journey inspire others. Remember that you have the power within you to make a difference – not only in your own life but in the lives of those around you. You never know whose life you may touch or whose dreams you may ignite by simply sharing your story. The world is waiting to be inspired by you.

Sharing Your Story and Experiences

We all have a unique story to tell, filled with experiences that have shaped us into who we are today. Our journey is a tapestry of triumphs, challenges, and moments of self-discovery. In the subchapter, "Sharing Your Story and Experiences," we will explore the power of embracing your personal strengths and igniting your passions through the act of storytelling.

Sharing your story is not only a way to express yourself but also a means of finding the good within you. It allows you to reflect on your experiences, uncover your strengths, and discover what truly ignites your passions. By sharing your story, you create an opportunity for self-growth, self-acceptance, and connection with others.

First and foremost, it is essential to embrace the uniqueness of your journey. No two stories are alike, and that is what makes each one so valuable. Recognize that your experiences, whether big or small, have shaped you into a person with a unique perspective and set of strengths. Embrace these qualities and understand that they are what make you special.

Once you have embraced your story, it is time to share it. Sharing your experiences can be a transformative and empowering process. It allows you to reflect on your journey, gain new insights, and find meaning in your experiences. By telling your story, you not only inspire others but also inspire yourself. Sharing your story can help you realize the resilience, courage, and passion that reside within you.

Remember, your story has the power to impact others. By sharing your experiences, you create a sense of connection and empathy with those who may have faced similar challenges. You never know how your story might inspire someone else to embrace their own strengths and passions. Your vulnerability can be a source of strength for others.

In conclusion, sharing your story and experiences is a powerful tool for finding the good within you. Embracing your personal strengths and igniting your passions through storytelling allows for self-growth, self-acceptance, and connection with others. Your story is unique and valuable, and by sharing it, you have the potential to inspire and empower not only yourself but also those around you. So, embrace your journey, reflect on your experiences, and let your story be a beacon of strength and inspiration for all.

Mentoring and Supporting Others

Mentoring and Supporting Others: Empowering the Good Within You

In the journey of self-discovery and personal growth, one of the most fulfilling and transformative experiences is mentoring and supporting others. When we extend a helping hand to those around us, we not only enhance their lives but also unleash the power within ourselves. This subchapter delves into the importance of mentoring and supporting others, highlighting how it can help us find the good within ourselves.

At its core, mentoring is about sharing knowledge, wisdom, and experiences to guide others on their path towards success and fulfillment. By becoming a mentor, we tap into our own strengths and passions, enabling us to ignite the same fire in others. As we invest time and energy in someone else's growth, we also discover untapped potential within ourselves.

Supporting others goes hand in hand with mentoring. It involves providing encouragement, offering a listening ear, and being a source of strength during times of adversity. When we support others, we create a ripple effect of positivity that not only impacts their lives but also nourishes our own sense of self-worth and purpose.

One of the remarkable aspects of mentoring and supporting others is that it doesn't require any special qualifications or expertise. Every one of us possesses unique strengths and experiences that can benefit someone else. It could be as simple as lending a sympathetic ear to a friend or offering guidance to a coworker facing challenges. By recognizing the good within ourselves, we can inspire and uplift others, creating a powerful network of support and growth.

When we mentor and support others, we gain a deeper understanding of our own strengths and weaknesses. Through this process, we become more self-aware, learning to appreciate our talents and identify areas for improvement. Mentoring and supporting others also allows us to develop essential skills such as empathy, active listening, and effective communication, which are invaluable in both personal and professional relationships.

As we embrace the journey of mentoring and supporting others, we must remember that it is a two-way street. Just as we offer guidance and support, we also learn from the experiences and perspectives of those we mentor. This mutual exchange of knowledge and ideas enriches our own lives, further fueling our personal growth and passion.

In conclusion, mentoring and supporting others is a transformative practice that enables us to find the good within ourselves. By investing in the growth and well-being of others, we unlock our own potential, cultivate self-awareness, and foster meaningful connections. Whether it is within our families, workplaces, or communities, mentoring and supporting others is a profound way to embrace our personal strengths and ignite our passions.

Encouraging Self-Discovery and Personal Growth

In today's fast-paced world, it is easy to get caught up in the chaos and lose sight of our true selves. We often find ourselves seeking validation and happiness from external sources, neglecting the inner strength and potential that lies within us. However, the key to a fulfilling and meaningful life lies in self-discovery and personal growth.

In this subchapter, "Encouraging Self-Discovery and Personal Growth," we will delve into the transformative process of finding the good within yourself. Regardless of your background, age, or circumstances, this chapter is addressed to everyone seeking to embark on a journey of self-exploration and unleash their untapped potential.

The journey of self-discovery begins with the realization that you are unique and possess inherent strengths and passions. It is about acknowledging and embracing your individuality, rather than conforming to societal expectations. By understanding your strengths and weaknesses, you can harness your abilities and work towards personal growth.

Self-discovery is not a linear process; it involves exploration, reflection, and a willingness to step out of your comfort zone. It requires you to ask yourself difficult questions and confront your fears and insecurities. Through introspection, you can uncover your true passions and interests, enabling you to pursue a path that aligns with your authentic self.

Personal growth is a continuous journey that requires dedication and perseverance. It involves setting goals, both short-term and long-term, and working towards self-improvement. By embracing challenges and facing adversity head-on, you can develop resilience and discover inner strengths you never knew existed.

This subchapter will provide practical tools and techniques to encourage self-discovery and personal growth. From journaling exercises to mindfulness practices, you will learn how to cultivate self-awareness, embrace your strengths, and ignite your passions. Through inspiring stories of individuals who have embarked on their own self-discovery journeys, you will gain insight and motivation to embark on your own path of personal growth.

Remember, the power to transform your life lies within you. By taking the time to explore your true self, embrace your strengths, and ignite your passions, you can unlock your full potential and lead a fulfilling and purposeful life. So, grab a pen, open your heart, and embark on this transformative journey of self-discovery and personal growth.

Conclusion: Unleashing the Power Within You

In our journey through "The Power Within: Embracing Personal Strengths and Igniting Your Passions," we have explored the depths of self-discovery and witnessed the incredible potential that lies within each and every one of us. As we conclude this book, let us take a moment to reflect on the transformative power of finding the good within ourselves.

Throughout this journey, we have learned that finding the good within us is not about seeking validation from others or conforming to societal expectations. Instead, it is about embracing our unique qualities, strengths, and passions that make us who we are. It is about acknowledging our flaws and imperfections while understanding that they do not define us.

When we tap into our inner power, we unlock a world of endless possibilities. We discover the strength to overcome obstacles, the resilience to bounce back from failures, and the courage to chase our dreams relentlessly. It is through embracing our personal strengths that we can truly find our purpose and live a fulfilling life.

Each one of us possesses a set of talents and passions that are waiting to be unleashed. It is only by acknowledging and nurturing these strengths that we can reach our full potential. By doing so, we not only benefit ourselves but also contribute positively to the world around us.

Finding the good within you is not an easy task. It requires self-reflection, self-acceptance, and a commitment to personal growth. It requires letting go of self-doubt and embracing a mindset focused on possibilities rather than limitations. It is a continuous journey that requires patience and perseverance.

Remember, you are capable of achieving greatness. You have the power within you to make a difference in your own life and the lives of others. Embrace your strengths, pursue your passions, and never stop believing in your potential.

As we bid farewell to this book, let it serve as a reminder that the power within you is boundless. It is up to you to unleash it and embark on a path of self-discovery and personal growth. Embrace the good within you, and watch as it transforms your life in ways you never thought possible.

May you find the strength, happiness, and fulfillment you seek as you continue your journey of self-discovery. Remember, you are extraordinary, and the power within you is waiting to be unleashed.

www.ingramcontent.com/pod-product-compliance
Lightning Source LLC
LaVergne TN
LVHW051957060526
838201LV00059B/3701